THANH DINH

Salt & Ashes

Poems From the Abyss

First published by Writerly Books 2025

Copyright © 2025 by Thanh Dinh

All rights reserved. No part of this publication may be reproduced, stored or transmitted in any form or by any means, electronic, mechanical, photocopying, recording, scanning, or otherwise without written permission from the publisher. It is illegal to copy this book, post it to a website, or distribute it by any other means without permission.

Thanh Dinh asserts the moral right to be identified as the author of this work.

Thanh Dinh has no responsibility for the persistence or accuracy of URLs for external or third-party Internet Websites referred to in this publication and does not guarantee that any content on such Websites is, or will remain, accurate or appropriate.

Designations used by companies to distinguish their products are often claimed as trademarks. All brand names and product names used in this book and on its cover are trade names, service marks, trademarks and registered trademarks of their respective owners. The publishers and the book are not associated with any product or vendor mentioned in this book. None of the companies referenced within the book have endorsed the book.

First edition

ISBN: 978-1-0694998-2-0

This book was professionally typeset on Reedsy. Find out more at reedsy.com

*For the loss of my life. Sorry I was not the one you needed.
And you were never mine.*

Contents

Acknowledgments iii

I Andante

The Louki Within	3
The Artist	4
In Reply to M.G.S.T.'s "Howl"	6
About Giving Up	9
Letter to M.	11
Feather	14

II Romanze

Keigo	19
The Things That Help You Sleep	23
Hiraeth	25
How Are You?	28
Pretend	30
Conversation With A Ghost	32
Rain	37

III   Scherzo

Reading Nam Cao in the Dark	41
Dumpster Politics	43
Street Cleaners	45
Sisyphus Must Be Happy	47
Dancing Queen	51
Shoot	54

IV   Finale

The Misfit – Or The Gospel of Judas	59
Decay	61
Truth	63
Truth Be Told	66
Didn't Know She Was Still Alive	68
Burn	70
Skin	73
Show Some Mercy	76
Praises for The Smallest God Who Ever Lived	78
About the Author	80
Also by Thanh Dinh	81

Acknowledgments

This work is not mine alone.

It is the combined product of my mother's endless encouragement, my sister's support, and my father's cheers from the other side of the Pacific Ocean.

And of course, my friends' toleration of my craziness when I call them at midnight, discussing ideas and laughing about my depression.

Also, this is the fruit of the people – doctors – who had and have been saving me from Death's door: Dr. Le Minh from University Medical Centre HCMC and Dr. Ton That Minh from Tam Duc Cardiology Hospital.

I wouldn't have survived without you.

As with all my works, the previous one and the next ones to be released after this, the gratitude will always be offered to my honored one: Professor Richard Greene from the University of Toronto Mississauga – Thank you for believing in my shallow talent.

Yes, this work is not mine alone. Nothing ever is.

SALT & ASHES

PART
— I —
ANDANTE

"It's enough for me to be sure that you and I exist at this moment."

– One Hundred Years of Solitude by Gabriel Garcia Marquez

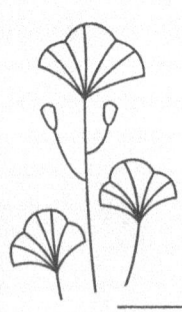

The Louki Within

Mulling over Patrick Modiano's "In the Cafe of Lost Youth"

A person once told me, "There are worse things in life than death."

I was younger then. I didn't quite understand how there could be anything more frightening than an ending. But there are. A plethora of them.

Be it Modiano's Paris, Miyazawa's Galactic Railroad, or all the other great works from the greater authors who the Nobel committee fails to recognize – they stand as a sacred testament for one thing: Being human means bearing a greater solitude in a solar system that will outlive all of us.

It means sometimes, you want to let yourself go like the lonesome and pretty Louki in Modiano's Paris.

It means, despite having a Louki within, you have to choose the living.

It means you have to suffer and find meaning in those sufferings.

It also means that there are beauties beyond the simple choice of being alive and being dead.

Like the flowers that bloom after the burning of Australia's forests, for example. Choose the living. Choose the spring.

The Artist

The light follows the artist in the dark –
    He is performing the last role in his grandiose career: the master
Of a farce –
A used-to-be –
A never-once-has-been –
A never-will-be-again –
And on this night, so lonely, so desolate in its quietude of the soft minuet of pain
He could cry for the grand finale:
The drag rehearsal for a special line
Of a man who would soon be gone.
Tattered clothes –
Wearied face –
Legs dragging behind him – oh, the shackled dreams
Of a fate he yearned to escape –
Though the bird has every right to fly,
Its wings grow tired –
And there comes a time when people learn
How futile living on pure imagination can be –
See, he used to believe
In the benevolence of God's embrace –

THE ARTIST

The laughter of the audience –
Their tears –
Their cheers –
Their standing ovation –
Wasn't it he who taught them the magic phrase:
It is possible to hope –
To have faith in the goodness of human – but
How can he know the strength within him
Can only carry the fever passion so far?
It pays to wish on a star – he understands it
And as he takes the last dance on the darkening stage,
He wonders through whose eyes the pain is shining
So brilliant, yet –
so bright, so cruelly desolate
it could kill the whole human race with a teardrop?
Look, he breathes, his voice quivering –
In the empty space of the theater, the curtains draw close,
The artist is –
Weeping.

In Reply to M.G.S.T.'s "Howl"

She was a provincial girl –
   not the kind of provincial girl you think –
   jewels and queendom and kings –
   and what-have-you from the well-to-do manors and castles –

   but it is fun to dream.

To see her, you must look harder
   between the thistles and weeds
   and the rattling shelters
   made from leftover dinners and broken dishes and lonely –
what?
   Hope.

She never gets anything better to do
   than to lose herself in the magic wonderland of imagination –

   who can tell the difference
   between the real and the fake?
   She came to your country purely by chance –
   a chance many deem hard to come by
   some even envy – the vice dresses between their teeth like a

fucking crown
   on the teaching Thou art no better than the suffer in us –
   The followers of the little faith called Hypocrisy.
   Glory be Thy name, whom we cannot judge.

She graduated from the top school – top of her class
   and burned her degrees to ashes when winter comes –
   accreditation, acknowledgment, big words don't bring dinners home.
   She thought a bookshelf full of dead men –
   and sometimes living ones –
   will make her a better person;
   too bad, old man Charles was drunk and said, "Don't try."
   Yet you ask her to let you hear her howl.

Who else talks about Nietzsche now?
   His words are great in their emptiness and great in their follies.
   And who would tell you about Hemingway?
   The machismo and the masochism in his writing –
   while you stand there thinking, *Did she even understand the two words she just spoke?*
   The uninvited, the unloved, the unchosen, the betrayed –
   in a way, you can say
   she has eaten so many leftover dinners so now, she slowly becomes one –
   the leftover that nobody wants.

Don't ask her to howl.
   Did you know she lost her voice a long time ago
   on a desert far, far away?

Did you know the only reason she stays
is to find a reason
to love living enough
to wake up another day,
to love the species enough
so she can love herself,
to simply be
so she won't have to ask the question of "not to be."
Hamlet. Act III Scene II.

After facing death, she finds the phantom of living so much more endurable.
Did you know that in her world, there are only two types of people –
the ones who used her and the ones who abandoned her –
she despises herself enough to love them all.
She doesn't want to go to Heaven because she wants to fall into the arms of the lost and the unchosen.
You ask to hear her howl, monsieur, and let me tell you, don't bother.
Her silence shakes the whole forest –
In her eyes, the night is ablaze with fever -
she is the fever dream
you only encounter once in a lifetime on a blue moon.
Dans la nuit, elle est femme devient fou

And when you see her again, perhaps later, perhaps soon,
Ask her then, and she will say unto you –
The nothingness that mortals fear more than death
Mais il est elle du amoureux. Toujour.

About Giving Up

She's a wolf.
 When the moon strikes at midnight and its blue light paints a shadow of pain,
she turns into this hideous creature
moving along the shops' windowpanes:
her claws leave red blood on the pavements, and her hair falls down the well;
is it her blood or someone else's?
And even if she knows the answer, will it make any difference?

She's a beast.
 Her heart grows as big as the old fairy tales.
 Perhaps when she was born, a witch left a curse on her.
 A curse that looks like a red claw mark of the wolf, looking at her:
 His yellow eyes still haunt her dreams.
 I will call you back, he said;
 I will check the message you left, he said;
 She doesn't know what to do when she hears words like that,
 because the wolf chases after freedom, and she was locked inside the prison she chose, hoping
 someone will release her from the loneliness of old.

She's the moon.
   Though there are hollow abysses and craters on her face,
   she still manages to ride through the waves,
   and when her beauty shines, once in a while, on the full moon night,
   she brings the silver ocean to his lover, the shore:
   She knows that now and forever more,
   there's no love for a moon that's a thousand hundred miles from it.

She's a girl.
   Broken and destroyed and rusty – you name it.
   She wasn't born this way, she promised you that,
   but the rest is as old as time, and she never mentions it.
   Of course, I know lies when I hear them, she said,
   but how can one give up on hope?
   And when she asks you that, you are stunned.
   You don't know if she can distinguish truths from fiction,
   or whether she sees through your facade.
   You wonder what she wants: loyalty or another hurtful breakup.
   Perhaps it will help your conscience when you know that
   she's been long used to both.
   I will call you back, you said,
   And I will check my mailbox more often, you said.
   She smiles through and through, *I know*.

She's a human.

Letter to M.

Dearest M.,
    Do forgive me for putting these words into verses
    Which will only complicate things –
None of us wants a fucking pedagogy;
But M.
Is there anything on this Earth that is ever
Complicated?

Dearest M.,
    I had a dream.
    I don't even know if it was about the me and you
    Or someone else –
    someone more unhappy –
    More painful, filled with undeserved sufferings, but
    The man was confessing his love and
    The woman says, *That's good, but I want to hear it again 100 years from now.*
    But darling, none of us will be alive
    100 years from now,
    He smiled at her, his loving gaze caressing her face
    with longing and solitude,
    But there's one thing you could do:

Just die before me.

You make that sound so simple, the woman giggles innocently.

Her beauty was in between and everywhere.

The man tucked her strand of hair gently behind her ear, and with sadness in his weary eyes, he said:

Darling, nothing in this world is ever that complicated.

And the dream ended.

I don't remember the first half of it, but I presume

Like all things had happened, it must have been a happier scene:

Where the lovers were not so old and

Desperate and – what?

hopeless.

Dearest M.,

If it's not visible in the retelling of my dream

It must be visible here:

I don't want to wait for 100 years –

the wars are rolling in and who knows?

The God is onto us. Maybe one day I will wake up,

when life is better, when people declare peace

because there is none left to kill –

which means you are no longer here.

I had to mourn the death of my love for you

In front of a grave that cannot speak and

A soul I cannot see.

Whatever I ever said and

Whatever I wanted it to be between us

Had long gone.

A Houdini act minus the laughing entertainment.

Because M., none of us will be here 100 years from now,

And nothing on this Earth will be that complicated.

Feather

Feverish fingers dance on porcelain skin,
    leaving behind them the touch of scorching passion –
    Bruising kisses –
Wet tongues on dry lips –
Someone forgot to tell Joan of Arc
She was dead –
The stake burns through the night
And the flesh comes ablaze –
Living has never been so bright in all its writhing malice –
And while she breathes through the misery,
The fingers stealthily slip through her leatherette strap –
Burn, burn, this agonizing thirst –
Where is the love that is rumored to cure all sufferings that could be?
And you can hear the quivering voice of her smoldering desire escape –
    Through close lips, tongue-tied, her head turns,
    she whispers his name to the endless void
That once was her existence:
I thought you were mine –
Spelling out the pain, soft as feathers falling on skin –
Before the Earth moves,

the feverish fingers keep trailing on her skin,
Leaving behind a map of the wasteland –
The country every stranger wishes to visit
But none yearns to stay –
Leaving is just another trait of human nature –
And who is she to wage a war against the system?
Raindrops on spring leaves –
Like playing a sonata from centuries of old
the cold sound of the piano keys thumping on the eardrums –

She watches the rain fall on the petals of the cherry blossom –

The snow melted, burying a part of her in the dream of him. Yet –
Something was born of darkness, and something
was born of truth.
Her lips whisper his name again when the winter thunderstorm strikes
and in her heart, carnage is the sovereign.
How she wishes she could feign
Ignorance
and pretends to be
Vices dressed in
Innocence.
Feverish fingers. Blazing skin –
quivering lips, tongue-tied, silk dress slips through the cracks of the first dawn –
Remember that only in the aftermath of the quake,
You can feel the Earth move.

SALT & ASHES

PART
—— II ——
ROMANZE

Lying, the telling of beautiful untrue things, is the proper aim of Art.

– The Decay of Lying by Oscar Wilde

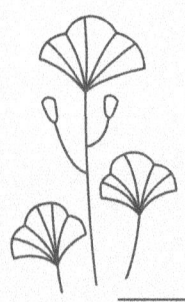

Keigo

I heard you changed your job again.
　　I thought I had known you better than to believe in the nonsense you make
about promises and the oath to be by each other's side, despite the earthquake
that is sweeping across the land, and darling, the Babel Tower
had long fallen, so if you come to me in full armor and ask me
"What are you talking about?"
I would still understand.
I heard you needed me -
just like you need another piece on your chessboard to win against life.
I think I would cry, but who knows that you have long pushed me past the point of pity.
I ask you if you have read Shakespeare
and if you have known about Hamlet,
and you tell me you are ready to listen to everything I say
as long as I pay for it.
Thus, I don't have the chance to tell you about Ophelia,
about how she goes crazy after Hamlet kills her father
and her love for him is so strong that it pushes her over the

lake
  and she dies in the coldness of winter.
  But of course, I am not Ophelia.
  You always tell me that I am stronger than you are.
  Darling, it would take much more than strength and courage alone
  to send a message in a foreign language across the ocean
  hoping that the person who receive it will find hidden among the nonsense
  something akin to love.
  I burn the scarf I knitted for you just to watch the last sparkles of your voice
  die out on my skin
  and carve out the map of Japan.
  Amidst the pain and the silent cry, I can point out on my skin
  the shape of Tokyo and your smile.
  "You are so kind," you often say, "So why,
  why would you ever need me?"
  You put so much contempt in kindness as if to point out to me
  that kindness does not feed the poor, and certainly,
  it does not make money grow on trees.
  Darling, of course, I see how my kindness kills me.
  In the sleepless nights, I can feel kindness tower over me like the final Titan that Zeus cannot kill –
  even Atlas cannot bear its weight; so he shrugs, and the Earth crumbles to pieces.
  Who are we to think our ending would be different?
  I pick up whatever is left of my kindness and crush it in the palm of my hand
  just to feel the beating of Life's heart.

Isn't it wonderful to know that
Life will burst under the touch of a feather?
You know, I'd rather be Ophelia.
In the heart of darkness, did you ever hear the rattling breathing of the kindness
you wish to kill?
Perhaps Ophelia heard its whisper, and like the moth be to the flame,
she sunk deeper into the lake, hoping that kindness would warm
her unclaimed corpse.
Cruel, yes, but one can imagine that in the last hour of flickering hope,
Ophelia was happy.
See? It's just nonsense. A make-believe ending. Promises
that I lay down on the foundation of the fallen Babel Tower,
hoping that in the spring or summer,
when the last snowflake of winter melt away
in the bosom of the lake where Ophelia lay,
I can build a bridge across the ocean – and dear, wouldn't it make you –
hold onto hope and the living?
I heard you changed jobs again.
I thought I had known better than to believe in anything that life has to offer.
But God crushed humans' ambition, and Atlas shrugs,
so what else can salvage me from digging up the dirt with my bare hands
only to scream your name into the void
and bury the sound of my voice into the nothingness of Life's beginning?

I roll each syllable of your name on the tip of my tongue
and taste the frozen snowflakes of last winter.
The cherry blossoms bloom, and it will soon be another summer,
but your name is forever here, carved deep in the tissues of my flesh
and on a silent night, you can hear my bones creak; in their breath,
I can hear them say, "That's it, just let yourself go."
And perhaps it would make you happy to know
that like Ophelia, I long to jump into the frozen ocean,
only to taste the bitterness of your cigarette smoke
vanishing into the Tokyo night sky like a broken dream.
Ah, ma chérie, c'est trop oppressif
Apres tout, dans la nuit
On deviennent fou. Fou.

The Things That Help You Sleep

To my unknown lover and our little joke. I will forever remember you with the not-so-authentic phrase, Je suis mermaid.

After a while, you don't even know what is helping you sleep.
Be it a woman's embrace or a man's embrace -
what's the difference?
You sit on your chair and wear your tin-foil hat,
singing about the fairies and the flat-earth believers.
Perhaps once, in a fever dream of dying childhood
and unclaimed future,
you had wanted to believe that the earth was flat
so that you could reach the other side faster.
After a while, you don't know if you're reading a book
or drinking a cup of warm tea -
you just know that you did *something*,
but what is that *something*? You can't tell.
All you understand is: It helps you move on.
Continue the fight.
Existing. Until one day, you won't. Can't
As you lie on the soft mattress of sorrow, staring at the ceiling.
The fan seems like it is living, but is it?
The light seems like it is burning, but is it?

And you seem like you are living –
but are you?
After a while, you know that sleeping includes closing your eyes,
but you don't know what happens after that.
Is it dreaming? Have you ever gotten as far as dreaming?
Is it darkness? Have you ever gotten as close as darkness?
Wait, have you taken the pills?
Or have the pills taken you?
After a while, you don't sleep.
You just get up and get on with it.
No matter what *it* is, you get on with it.

Hiraeth

I turn around, trying to find the place I belong –
    The road leading to that foregone home
    Has long been buried in the snowstorms
Of the many winters I ignored
and the many winters to suffer through.
For a person who favors nothingness,
I grasped onto the greed of the living
Far too hastily –

I turn around, the sound of the empty promises reverberated in my ears –
    The sweetest song I will ever hear.
    It says, *The defeat is drawing near* –
    And though that fact has been carved onto my body
    Like an ancient curse –
    a relic, forgotten, from the many centuries
    Of wars and peace –
    Yet the dying heart is still beating
    In my ribcage.
    How can one stop dreaming of the living
    And hoping for the dead?
    Outside, the cherry blossom is blooming –

I can show you the fervent prayers – kneeling at the altar
   Of a God I never believe in, screaming in His deaf ears:
   The Word is broken in between
   And broken when Thou art here.
   You see, I chase after the fleeting shadow of the hare
   On the dark side of the moon.
   My mind keeps saying, "Soon"
   And my heart keeps begging me, "Never."

Where are you in this unfathomable ocean
   when Existence is baring the sharp white teeth
   Ready to swallow the last shred of humanism?
   My feet
   Walk on water,
   but you who are so in love with freedom and refuse to acquiesce
   Should know that your wings can never bring you as far as
   The life you are living in.

I whisper your name – each syllable became so foreign
   That for a split of a second,
   Your face faded to ashes – whose corpse was I burning?
   The voice of many summers faraway
   Dripping into my ears like the sweetest nectar of the first batch of honey –
   I don't want you. I want all of you.
   Droplets of desire burn my skin, and as the panic is sinking in,
   I run blindly ahead – what are we, if not the arch-nemesis
   Of the right to be free?

HIRAETH

You are my hiraeth. And I, your forsaken ghost – the unlived life,
    The babe that breathes but only once before the weight of the world
    Crushed it.
    Look at us running in circles.
    One has to admire the effort we spend
    on burning each other at the stake of hatred.

I don't hate you. I hate all of you.
    I turn around, hoping that one day,
    Stumbling in the snow of this foreign country
    You will be there.
    Tell me a funny story.
    Tell me how you became my greatest defeat, my vainglorious victory –
    The wounds on the head, the pulse in the palms,
    The vanquished battle where I hold you in my arms –
    Tell me how to unfold the misery we are living in
    But don't let me forget you again.

How Are You?

A tribute to my mother in free verse. Hope it will be worthy of all her sacrifices.
   You lie awake at night,
as I lie next to you,
convulsing,
trembling,
wandering
in the land of the Death.
If I must be honest,
I was on the border when you turned around
holding me down
and ask me,
How are you?
Your "*how are you*" means a lot of things –
and what a coincidence, they are all sad things,
bad things,
mournful things.
How I wish to turn your "how are you" into something else.
I can't bear to see the years gone by on your face –
the years of being abused by your mother,
the years of being abused by your husband, and later on,
the years of sacrificing your freedom for the two children

who could barely support you now.
I'm fine, I wanted to say in my delirium,
but the convulsion and the deafening hallucination
is stopping my sanity from reaching you.
I'm fine, mother, I really am fine.
I never wanted to be a lunatic, mother, I never wanted it.

It was just right there on the border, and I happened to carry it with me

when I stared Death straight in the face and gave him the middle finger.

And mother, though you are still smiling,
your smiles grow wearier and wearier each year –
and I am scared of *the day* - the final moment.
All parties have to end, and I'm not allowed any regrets –
But if I am, mother, my biggest regret is
growing up to be nothing more than an idiot
who is both deaf and blind.
I'm a lunatic, mother, I have always been
since the day I was still inside your womb.
But you see me dying and you pull me through –

Mother, you have become my sanity – whatever sanity that is left within me,

and I'm sorry, mother,
I can never be whatever you want me to be.

Pretend

You say when you are walking out the door
    that you will be back home when the tide hits the
    shore, and honey,
I don't know if I should believe in you or
if I should believe in Schrodinger's cat:
Whether you will be home or not, I won't know
until the box is opened. Hey –
Did you know that in Schrodinger's experimental condition,
the cat would end up dead?

You say you are lonely, and to be honest,
    I should take that as a hint to leave because
    no sane person would see the abyss and think to themselves,
That's a nice place to die.
But darling, I am the kind of person who
always dream of something crazy.
The kind of person
who will bury Schrodinger's cat –
who understands that whether you come back or not:
it doesn't matter.
Holding onto hope is a human condition
because what else do we have besides hoping

when everything is falling apart?

You say when you walk out the door
    that you will be back soon, and furthermore,
    we will get married.
    But darling, seeing the suitcase in your hand,
    and the ticket of the flight you are taking,
    I know better than to believe in
    the abyss,
    the hopes,
    Schodinger's cat,
    and the empty promises
    you left onto the sweet lips of the darlings you meet –
    Que tu est belle –
    Ah, mon amoreux, c'est paroles, paroles –

Conversation With A Ghost

I look at her, shimmering in the air
    her hair made of silvery fog and smoky rare diamonds
    – blinding
But for whose eyes?
The witnesses are long gone –
I can see her in my utmost beautiful yet poignant memories
–
When the pain grew too high for me
And the love she sacrificed her soul to see it bloom
Into the immense field of withering lilies –
Hark, didn't you hear the moon howl –
The suffering has just begun –
Humans have always been – what?
Short of – what?
Cruel? No.

Just give them a chance.
    She breathes, and the dust in the last glimmering light of day
    quivers in the air ever so briefly, just so they could land again
on the table surface.
    She says, Do you ever think about faith
    And goodness?

and I say, Nietzsche thinks about it –
Albert Camus thinks about it –
Dostoyevsky thinks about it –
Hell, Charles Bukowski thinks about it;
He said, Knowing about life, one would think that we should love each other more
but instead – what?
and she digresses, It's always the same.
We talk a lot of nonsense
just to try to define a thing so meaningless we could cry wolf,
and do you think it just – what? – useless
to end our sentences with "but instead," "and yet," "nonetheless"?

I don't really care what Charles Bukowski said;
But what if you did, I insist,
And what if I didn't, she resists –
to her, it is just another temptation to argue with a stubborn head
Another Sisyphus leading a life she does not know yet
and neither does she care to learn more because she couldn't care less
about the life of the past and the life of the future –
she is stuck inside, a prisoner of her own free mind
To her Sisyphus must be happier since he will always know what lies yonder
on the horizon of a new tomorrow - a new sorrow, sweet and tender.

But this is not about her, or me, or anyone else for that matter –

She picks up the strand of invisible hair
shining in the moonlit air - how long have I been sitting here
by her side and by the sideline of the road, burdened with blood and stones
that ghosts like her had gone and left behind
as a token of their strong will - a determination of the mind
that never again shall they be ghosts wandering in the night?
Why are you at my side? She asks, and suddenly
the thunderstorm blasts. The rain has come when nobody is sad enough for it –
Still she insists, Why,
and I resist, Perhaps because I want to see you, the only one living while everyone is dying -
because a thousand reasons why will not be sufficient to bury the hatchet
and the sound of killing roars from the pit of mass graves and unnamed tombstones
like the Howitzers are still alive after so many wars have been fought and many soldiers fall -
perhaps because I see your sorrow -
you are waiting for the ones that will never come back tomorrow.

You know how deep promises are, I tell her,
   They dig up trenches to guard themselves
   against the broken promises
   like how they guard themselves against enemies and wars –
   I wonder how many people the promises have buried
   and how many more will fall down the trench, unhurried.
   She resists, I make no such promises –
   unlike you, I don't feed on dreams and live on a bed of roses

– and so

  I must wonder why you are here

  Amidst the piers for the last boats –

  Everyone is leaving, what makes you think you won't be like the rest? She says,

  You are damn near starvation if I ever see a starving person –

  don't you hear that your dreams are dead, and they are creating a new monument?

  I guess it is only fair then, I say to her, that I should become a ghost – like you, chasing after

  The hunger for love and what could have been –

  For something better, because life can always offer it –

  and what are you saying about the last one standing?

  I saw him fall long ago - amidst the ocean -

  he died without a warning,

  not from starvation but from the faith of hopeless believers –

  and you should have seen him then; he was nothing but a skeleton

  of the things that "had-been" and the things that will be "never-again."

I see her cry. I hear her moan –

  A single teardrop for the man who died without a blanket to cover the life he led.

  The last one standing, I say, Can one always stay in the past and live in the future?

  No one stays in the past and no one lives in the future, she replies, looking out at the stormy ocean –

  The sky is bleak with the death of our endings –

  Go on, then, find yourself, she urges,

  And maybe when you see her, you will find out

Who your arch-nemesis has always been? What?
Is it strange that
She wears the same face
As you?

Be human first, then come back here,
   And stay on this Earth
   As the rightful ghost that you are born to be.
   After all, you are destined for me
   As a punishment.

Rain

I thought we would go out today, he says,
  but instead, we are staying home and watching a boring TV show,
and listening to the sound of the pouring rain outside –
Are you out of your mind?
He curls into a ball on my lap, spilling his complaints
the same way a bartender spills his liquor:
without reservation, and without a care whether the customer
will be able to tolerate the heat from the strong spirit.
I would prefer staying home, I say.
Like how you prefer to leave the curtains down, he says,
when the sun is out –
or like that other time: you would prefer to stay by my side
in the emergency room,
listening to my delirious talk and crying over my bleeding wrist.
Yes, my darling, yes.
Do you prefer to suffer?
No, my darling, no.
I simply prefer having you by my side
than being alone on my own.
And when being drowned is the only option for you,
I would prefer to drown with you, too.

He looks at me, laughing, *You are weird*,
then he hides his face into my bosom,
It's strange. It's not soft. It's not like my mother's.
He buries his head deeper into the hard muscles on my stomach,
his tears form a wet circle on my T-shirt.
I stroked his silky black hair. It's comforting to think that I will see his black hair
Turns white.
You know what, darling, I say,
What?
I would prefer staying home on rainy day,
like I would prefer skipping my breakfast,
or like how I would prefer putting my shoes in the exact same place
I put them in the previous day,
or like -
Like what? He mumbles in his drowsy sleep.
I wait to hear his shallow breathing,
and as his hands lose their grip on my ribcage, I whisper:
Like I would prefer having you. More than anything.
I would prefer having you. Loving you. Living with you.
It's all you, you, you.
Darling, you smell like the rain,
and though I can choose to be out in the sun,
I would always prefer the rain –
we are not the only ones
being abandoned.
There's no argument. No insult. No tantrum.
There's only the me who is holding on,
and the you who is letting go.

SALT & ASHES

PART
— III —
SCHERZO

"Rise up, please! A woman was not born to be a slave!"

– Nam Cao

Reading Nam Cao in the Dark

Nam Cao said, The system created the man –
　　Who would understand the words he laid down –
　　Black ink on white paper
As the night of the past has grown far to thin
To dictate the way of the future –
I wonder what the man sees in the dank, low rental room,
His eyes glazed over,
His mind was a quiet rot –
The ideals chase him to victory but the hunger thinks not –
And he laments the lost of his life –
More human than any other human who has ever graced this Earth, Yes, he said, The system created the man.

Nam Cao said, Rise up, for the women are not born to be a slave –

Fifty years later, the women he wrote about still suffer –

The silent sacrifice screams louder with each passing generation –

A virtue? Nay, a lost cause disguised as the most celebrated trait in a female protagonist –

She was born to be taken advantage –

And he knew, but what did it matter?

She chose to be destroyed –

Until she realized no matter how much she laid down her life for it,

That society won't bother to look back

And see her for who she is: a human –

An equal –

A soul –

An existence.

Nam Cao said, Goodness must be earned –

But he also asked, What have you done to deserve goodness?

Holding onto hope because hope is the only thing left –

You are rotting without smelling the stench of your own decaying flesh –

Waiting for salvation –

Thinking God will listen –

Praying and forgetting what you pray so fervently for –

Trusting that you deserve goodness, because once in a blue moon

You drop a silver coin in a beggar's hat –

Go buy a lottery ticket

So you can sleep on the dream of becoming filthy rich –

Don't you see the stupidity in your darkness?

Nam Cao said – Nay, it is you who said it first:

Rise up – you are not born to be a slave.

Dumpster Politics

He sits on the makeshift throne built from broken bricks
And rotting trash, counting his days of sovereignty –
The wasteland opens underneath his feet –
To flee or not to flee, nay –
His subjects are screaming for a new form of entertainment
And he is not one to refuse the sweet indulgence of hatred and seething vengeance –
They are not us –
Blessed be the sentiment upon which his kingdom comes.
The question falls as his gavel hits the tin can –
To kill or not to kill –
He revels in the glorification of any feasible reason
To induce fear –
Anger –
The scale tips one point further –
The feather falls, heavy as the thunderstorm that broke the Babel Tower
And in the madness of insatiable hunger,
The beast in him roars alive, swallows in its wake
The children –

The women –
The past –
The future –
Leaving behind a barren future
As lonely as the last human on Earth.
His people trust in the crown made from green paper –
Treasury Bills –
Executive Orders –
Decrees –
Big words for the smallest man who ever lived.
All the while, the wheel of history keeps crushing the forgettable life
Of the fleeting race –
How fragile is an existence
That could end itself on the terms
"Conflict of interests"?
Choose, he says, his body shackles down the freedom that was once paid up front
With blood –
Flesh –
And sheer will to power –
An ideology summarized in three words;
We the people –
Choose, he says.
And hopefully, when the people rise up this time,
The dumpster will be on the right side of history.

Street Cleaners

I saw a street cleaner swiping his whole body into the garbage truck, and the image of his half corpse, half nothing but blood and soft flesh, stuck in my mind like a giant baobab tree with its roots covering the entire Earth. The world moves on like a man's life has never been lost, and since the beginning of time, I have often wondered what kind of God would allow such barbarity. Suffered children, come unto me, He said. Did he know that thousands of years from then, those exact words are used to lure children to nothing but a net of death, darkness, the predators' disguise as sweetness? *Suffered children, come unto me* - I find it funny, but of course, I am an atheist. The cruelest crusade I have ever mounted against him is to prove to my elementary teacher that the Earth is round, and it revolves around the sun. He was never there when the first human walked upon the baked earth after the last rain, and He will never be there when the corpse of the last human turns into sand. I saw a street cleaner - or to be more exact, I saw half of a street cleaner stuck in the garbage truck - and I cannot help but wonder, *What kind of God is looking down on this street cleaner and deciding that he shall not live forever? How about his wife, his children, his dreams, and the unattainable happiness he chases after? Not anymore*, He dictates, *Not anymore*; you must suffer before you come to the shore. But God, look yonder, Your children are crying. The wounding of bombs and wars and guns and what You have opened for mankind with a spark of fire will not heal. The Earth is scarred, and yet You are sitting on your throne made from golden corpses and gilded horns, laughing. *Suffered children, come unto me.*

Sisyphus Must Be Happy

I stand on the rooftop of my towering childhood, thinking,
    Has anyone ever talked about the stone
    Sisyphus was bearing?
The wind is blowing through my scanty hair. It's high noon.
I can feel the sharp razor edge cut my chest wound open,
And my heart lies there bleeding, palpitating –
Like the wings of a butterfly, dying without living.

I often think about Sisyphus and his stone of sins,
    About how he cannot give up,
    About how everything he does will turn to dust,
    About his Hell,
    About the punishment,
    About how every one of us is living like a special Sisyphus
    In our private bubble of punishment –
which we often mistake for happiness.
Is it a blessing?
Living a life knowing that there will be another tomorrow,
and another. And another.
Or is it a curse? Knowing that there's no ending –
We are simply running in a circle?

The sun is gone.
   The noon changes to night –
   And if I were half sane, I'd think it's nice enough
   Just to live.
   After all, you cannot kill a person twice, and I already died.

I stand on the rooftop of my towering childhood, thinking,
   All it takes is to jump down.
   But I know the next moment I open my eyes,
   I will be on the rooftop,
   Again and again and again.
   The Void said, *Dying is easy*,
   But She never faced death.
   Instead, She faces me –
   The epitome of broken wishes and futile dreams.
   I am the closest thing to death, I said,
   Why?
   Because I've been living in repeat mode.
   I can count the number of lives I've been through
   With my two hands –
   Even so, I can't cross the barren desert of this never-ending land –
   The road is winding –
   And every step is another second I sink deeper
   In this hurt.
   This dream of many dreams,
   And this montage of many vintage films.
   I told her that counting is easy, you just have to add the one to the other.
   The numbers belong to the sphere of another species –
   But not to me.

One, two, three, one, two, three,
Who says that Sisyphus must be happy?

I stand on the rooftop of my towering childhood, staring down,
   Below is darkness and the corpses I've drowned
   To be me.
   I push down the stone, one after another,
   But the corpses keep on piling up, one after another,
   And the sins keep coming back, one after another.
   I turn to my accomplice, the man on the slope,
   The King of all Kings,
   The sin of all sins,
   I ask him, *Have you ever been happy?*
   He pushes the stone down the peak; *Must I be happy?*
   I don't know, I said,
   Because a man once said,
   To live a life like that, one must imagine that Sisyphus must be happy.
   And was that man happy? Sisyphus asked.

I stand on the rooftop of my towering childhood, looking at the man
   climbing down the slope,
   Again and again and again.
   The sharp razor edge plunges deep into the wings of the butterfly –
   I die for the thousandth time that night –
   In the bottomless well of the living,
   Walking across the line of sanity and insanity,
   Thinking, *You must imagine that you must be happy.*
   Why?

Sisyphus knows the answer to that.

Dancing Queen

Sir, I took dancing to a new level,
   she says, dunking the last of her shots for today.
   Who knows, God forbid, if the shots tomorrow will be more or less
   than what she has now?
   And who knows, God forbid, what does it even matter to her?
Sir, I took dancing to a new level,
she says, as he wraps his weary arm around her.
The night is coming to a close, and neither he or she
has a place to return to.

Sir, is it true?
   What is? His voice blurs away in the blasting music.
   Is it true that apologies are born
   because no one can ever bear the responsibilities of their actions?
   Sir, tell me, what does an apology mean to you?
   Does it mean forgiving and forgetting?
   Does it only mean forgiving?
   Or does it have no meaning at all?
   He leans in – the smoke in between builds a thin foggy curtain,
   separating two vengeance souls.
   I don't know, he says, *What does it mean to you?*

Is it why you take dancing to a new level?

They smile as she takes off her last piece of clothing,
Sir, that's not it. I took dancing to a new level because all my life,
I always wanted someone to stay,
and all I ever had was someone walking away.
And sir, I took dancing to a new level because
The apologies always come too late –
But what does it have to do with me anyway?
You don't listen to an addict's spell and never buy a whore's sorry tales.

She wraps her legs around him –
the laughter perches on her lips like a bird ready to take fly
and the tears in her eyes are long dried –
There is no use crying over the many men
who will walk away after the night ends.

Sir, I don't like apologies. It means you will leave.
It means you think less of me.
It means less than a regret
and more like a farewell to a love you live on purchase.

In return, he whispers into her ears, soft with a sorrow he dares not let flow:
Me neither, little girl, me neither.

The music comes blasting in. The night sheds its withering breath.
Who among the lost souls on the dance floor
would last another mourning song from Edith Piaf?
The man won't know. But in the morning, he covers the corpse

of the dancing queen –

She wouldn't. Last.

Shoot

That's right, comrade, don't waver –
 On the battlefield, the truth is the first one to sacrifice itself
For the higher indifference, some call faith
And some call it by its real name, you will learn later
After your corpse is carried back home on my back –
Greed –
Vanity –
The side of human
Believing that they are more human
Than the rest –
That's right, comrade, shoot –
And don't stop, don't even hold your breath, don't think –
Pull the trigger –
Aim at the head of another person –
Never for one second imagine that he is your kin –
Your father –
Your son –
In another world, he might be your long-lost brother –
Is his blood any different?
Is his flesh made of stone?
Are his bones golden?

SHOOT

What have you not stolen from across the borderline of this fucking madness
Of the wars on endless death?
But, comrade, don't falter in your steps –
Even if you surrender now, it won't help –
Someone else will kill him in your stead, and perhaps
You will be next –
That's right, comrade, shoot –
Don't think –
Don't open your eyes –
Don't stare at the set of humans across the line –
Because once you do that
The truth will survive –
And you don't want something that grotesque
That ugly –
That haunting and macabre –
To massacre the winning side of history –
So, shoot, comrade, shoot.

SALT & ASHES

PART
— IV —
FINALE

THE TEARS OF THE WORLD ARE A CONSTANT QUANTITY. FOR EACH ONE WHO BEGINS TO WEEP SOMEWHERE ELSE ANOTHER STOPS. THE SAME IS TRUE OF THE LAUGH.

- WAITING FOR GODOT, SAMUEL BECKETT

The Misfit – Or The Gospel of Judas

He said, Who is the best human –
    Considers himself the best human –
    Come stand before me.
The people were silent –
They thought, who among them is not the best?
Best merchants –
Best salesmen –
Best liars –
And when it comes to the worst of the lot –
The best believers.
He said, Come stand before me.
They resisted, We fear –
And trembling –
Because you are no mere human.
He said, You will lead the cattle to the wrong altar –
There's no God on the suffered throne
Construed from your hypocritical cries
And resurrected through your tales –
Live a long life, then, and see
How the world unfolds to fit your narrative.
They said, But you are the Son.
And amidst all this commotion –

The anger, the accusations, the tolerated smile
Of accepted defeat –
The misfit stands up from his place, simply watching –
Stray from the path of right, because there is no right from the beginning –
Forced inside the frame because it's easier to have a villain
Inside a mortal story –
A tragic, heroic comedy –
The misfit walked up to the master, saying, I know from whence you came
I know the place you will return to –
You are no son of man, as you are no Son of Him –
And you are right, He wasn't all benevolent –
But I chose to serve my Master, and though a perfect human I am not –
I'm trust that I have been
a loyal servant.
Thus said, the misfit released his Master of the material realm –

No name for him, and the shame - the shame is boundless –
Dying is easy, his Master taught, but suffering through –
And you will see, this world that He builds
Were never meant for people with hearts
As light as yours.
The misfit wrote it down – The Gospel of Judas –
No one will live to tell the tales
And his suffering ends at last.

Decay

The curtain draws –
 The stage is closing –
 The finale is breathing its last rattled dying heartbeat
Through its palpitating pain
As the palms of the actors and actresses are outstretched –
Begging –
Praying –
For just one more second
Of that glorious light, shining into their glimmering eyes from the darkening ceiling –
Life is a grandiose scheme of predestined roles –
Someone please let the master puppeteer go home –
The silent auditorium –
The flame is gone –
Who will still be here when tomorrow comes?
Hush, the night in this abandoned theater is long –
And didn't you hear? They are trying to build another theater out there in space
Another place to die –
No life is remembered, and they are doing a good job at forgetting –
Who are they? The Fool asks in a quiet slumber,

The puppeteers, the leading roles say,

Because, unlike us, who have nothing to lose,

They fear falling into the abyss

After Death.

Who are they? The Fool asks again, quite confused by the multitude of voices.

The puppeteers, the leading roles cry,

They built the Babel Tower to reach God

But they did not know the mercy when God created the first human as a monster –

Tell them, Love one another –

They hear, Kill the other side –

The different ones –

The lost –

The forgotten –

As the orchestral music hits the crescendo, the audience shuffles to their feet –

The theater is empty –

The stage retreats once again to darkness

Until the next act goes on –

New actors and actresses

Born from a new set of humans –

They need the Divine Comedy to go on

They need –

Who are they? The Fool asks, his eyes vacant,

Quite lost in his childlike innocence –

A requirement for his role, total abandonment of all things vain and suffered –

The puppeteers, the void echoes back

From the nothingness where the last human on Earth lay, decaying.

Truth

Someone once said, *The truth is beautiful* –
   What they meant was, *History is beautiful* –
   Like the wars their country won –
The battlefields might be bloody, sure,
And the corpses unclaimed –
The families of the dead soldiers
Couldn't grieve or mourn –
Don't shed a tear –
For the country needs every little flesh and bone you can offer –
   Pain is a valuable currency –
   When all else fails, we can use suffering to trade for the blood of our enemies –
   Bargaining –
   A smart man will one day say, It's the art of the deal.

But the truth is beyond beauty and grotesque: no –
   And history is not a pageant queen –
   It doesn't teach us lessons –
   Right or wrong, what does it matter
   To a wheel whose sole purpose is to keep on crushing human life

And fate?
Did the Holocaust happen?
I hope a thousand years from now, the answer will still be yes.

Because a civil war is labeled as liberation –
Fighting for independence is classified as invasion –
Oppression is a form of making a country great again –
How can I complain? I'm living along the flow of history and it doesn't allow me to look sideways:
It forces me to watch things unravel –
Empires rise and fall –
Wars against death and wars against peace –
When I thought I had learned it all, history came back to me and told me that
The truth has changed:
The victors have overwritten what I have known –
Right and wrong –
Good and evil –
The winner and the vanquished –
Whose side has more dead people? Let them be the villain.

Righteousness. A good cause. For the people.
Empty words running on the engine of something so rotten and beautiful
Like the truth.
Seeing the corpses of those meaningless destruction burned on my skin –
A fucking scar no peace or sacred offering to the benevolent faithless God could heal –
I started to think, *Well, maybe the truth is*

TRUTH

There is a cruel beauty in Death.

Truth Be Told

that people believe more in sadness than in happiness -
   it's an age-old knowledge and sadness
   is contagious.
Sip a little from this cup of bitterness that we call life
and let's see if you can escape the whirlwind
of hopelessness and despair -
and why do you still love every bit of it?

Truth be told
   that a long time ago
   when God created Adam
   He has prepared Himself for betrayal -
   and why do you expect Him to love
   when His love has long been exhausted?
   Between cut-wrist and tongue-tied dead field of vast silence
-
   among the lamentations of the human
   toiling over life and toiling to reach an end,
   you can hear of His revenge.
   Do you expect me to see Him as a God of Mercy, then?

Truth be told,

that He cares not for fame or glory -
among the battlefields and the wars of victory,
He walks among the lighted torches, the human corpses,
and the blazing fire of the winners,
His last words before rising to Heaven,
If your lifespan were that short,
why don't you spend it on something or than loving each other?
and what's use would it be, to what end?
Or do you just want a page in history dedicated to you
and the pains you caused
like how you petrified and crucified Me before?
Why do you always want more
and for as long as the tides come to meet the shore,
you always come to Me when nothing else work -
Do you believe in Me or miracles -
fake and useless and dark as the Catacombs of Paris
built upon death, but nevertheless -
the miracles bring you happiness;
fleeting, yes, and disguises as white lies on a dark canvas
of desperation and an abyss of hopelessness.
He breaths the final exhausted breath
and disappears before the light reaches Earth -
you can see his haggard shadow imprinted in the mountains
and in your heart - have you noticed
how He sings in His loneliness?

Truth be told,
   He was dead, a long time ago.

Didn't Know She Was Still Alive

Didn't know she was still alive, my mother says.
>*Who?* I ask, and see a brief change of time on my mother's face.

The brief change of time that destroyed all the condominiums and office buildings
>that are starting to surround the city
>like lead poisoning.
>The brief change of time that brings back piece by piece,
>brick by brick,
>dust by dust,
>the neighborhood that my mother grew up in.

It certainly was not a happy neighborhood
>as a pain expression clouds my mother's face.
>*She was my friend's mother*, she says,
>*I wonder where all my friends are now: they all suffered a war
>that they took no part in and never wished for.*
>*It's better than father's friend*, I tell her,
>*they all died.*
>*Is it really better, though?* My mother says.

There was a slight quivering undertone as if she meant to say

That I was wrong.
That nothing is ever better than death.
That suffering a war is, sometimes, not an honor.
Is war an honor? If it were not, why did so many leaders choose to start it?
My mother didn't answer. She was lost
in the neighborhood where no one grew up to be happy.

Didn't know she was still alive, my mother repeats.
And in that simple repetition, my mother brings back with her
the magic of life: we all suffered a war,
and we all survived.

Burn

I remember telling you about Joan of Arc -
    about how she sacrifices herself to the flame of Paris
    and how her white bridal dress turns into shards of glass
piercing through my veins as I look into your eyes
through the lenses of blurred memories.
I remember reading through your words to weave myself
a world of dreams - full of deceits and lies and non-existent promises –
    but a beautiful world nonetheless.

I confess
    I never consider waking up in the morning an option
    until you come and tell me that I can live the life of a butterfly
–
    continue dreaming and forgetting the rest
    because of all the things that happened to me, you are the beautiful mess
    that I never knew I needed but always knew I wanted.

I guess
    all I want to say is I want the pain –
    the pain of being burned in the Hell you create –

BURN

the Hell of the vainly selfless and the selfishly hopeless.
Your lies are eternally burned into my skin like the fever of a child
   in the sultry winter of the dark, cold Winter Wonderland.
   I hold onto the agony and the pain, thinking, This is life –
   This is living.

I reach out both of my hands toward the stake, begging –
   my eyes were blinded by the Christmas lights and the peppermint candies –
   through the frosted windows, I can see a happiness that is so close to me
   like a snowflake,
   and when it touches my fingertip,
   I can feel it melting into my being
   and into nothingness.

My lips quiver but I can't feel the tears -
   They are falling, falling, falling
   like the first snowflakes of spring.
   No one knows they are there
   but sometimes, people are reminded of their existence
   in a cold wind.

I remember telling you about Joan of Arc -
   but does it ever matter?
   I guess what I wanted to say was
   if you wanted to build a fire,
   to brighten the window light,
   to warm the love that you never had for everything that's living

and everything that's dying,
then I would be the first one to jump into the flame.

Honey, if you see me now –
my skin is blotched with scars that lead to the palpitating heart –
the stupid thing has always been beating for you.

Skin

I look at my wrist with the thick patch of skin cutting across the white surface
   and it looks back at me, saying, *Not yet.*

I hide my razor in a place no one can see - my head
   is full of dreams and miseries
   running side by side like two racing horses –
   sometimes, one of them cuts ahead, but I never know which one it is –
   which one will bring me more happiness, and which one will bring peace.

I push ahead with the word 'anyways', and each step I take
   cuts deeper into my skin than the scar on my wrist –
   everyone tells me it's brave to hit life in the face and bear the slit throats
   and the thick battered skulls –
   but nobody ever tells me that life has no face, and more often than not,
   you will end up with slit throats and battered skulls.
   A famous writer once sulked,
Those whom life cannot break, it kills.

How could he expect me to believe him when life kills him, too?

I sometimes think about the monsoon moon
   and the rain on the terrace of flooded rice paddies and the asphalt road
     leading to a place with leaden clouds, and soon,
   I see myself digging up dirt to build a mausoleum for the life that I had shoved away –
   they say, *She has gone astray;*
   you can only see the passing of her silvery ghost when the May rain falls
   on the tin roof, whispering in the summer leaves for all to hear:
   I am abandoned, forsaken, a heedless sacrifice for the things that are no longer borne
   a will to live.
   The moon looks at her and says that
   It's fine to leave - wherever you arrive,
   we will all be by your side. And I ask,
   Who are "we"?

I live in the singular reality,
   I look at the moon and say, *There is only one of you and one of me.*
   I seize my hands and feel the life I already gave away seeping through the cracks –
   I thought the armor I had was stronger than that.
   And the thick patch of skin on my wrist stares back in the cold, silent night –
   Not yet, not yet, not yet.

SKIN

You know, they said
    that God builds a special Hell and we call it Heaven on Earth -

    where each of us hides a razor blade in the brain and waits for the burst
    of a call to arms,
    of the piercing scream that penetrates the calm night,
    of the rain falling on tin roof,
    of the whisper in a conversation with monsoon moon -
    and we don't need proof that we live a life:
    we tie our shoes, pick up our razor blades, push ahead with an "anyways" -
    They said, *Not yet*, but do you know what life says?
    It says, *Here we go again.*

Show Some Mercy

Darling can you please show me some mercy
    and spare me your pity.
    I don't need your sweet tears,
and I don't need your kind words.
Darling, I don't have the same luxury to feel what they call empathy
but to me, is just plain old
pity.
And surely, darling, I am not privileged enough
to forgive and forget.
I wish I had more to give away
than just daily bickering and hourly bitterness.
I can count the number of times we were happy
with one hand.
And on the other hand, I can set ablaze
the curse of our love
with burning matches.
I know you could always be more than just a sufferer
of all the insults, swearing, and obnoxious bantering
that are the core of my being.
So show me some mercy, darling.
I didn't choose to be this way.

After all, I only have one option: to live.
I don't know when your love comes in as a compliment
to that option.
I can't return it, and I can't exchange it for something else.
Something like hatred and cold, and grudges.
I guess the whole point of these meaningless words
is to beg you to stay.
I'm a beggar on the street, whose life depends entirely on the generosity
of your mercy.
That's why show me some mercy, my darling,
and keep on loving me.

Praises for The Smallest God Who Ever Lived

⭐ *Joc – 5 Stars*

"Reads like a late-night conversation with a friend — poignant and authentic."

⭐ *Dina – 4 Stars*

"Not just poetry — a comfort for the heart. Beautiful and unforgettable."

⭐ *– 5 Stars*

"Full of emotion and mystery — resonates deeply with grief, love, and loss."

⭐ *Mia – 5 Stars*

"A perfect blend of sadness and hope. I was captured from the first poem."

⋆ *Damla – 5 Stars*

"Raw, loud, tender — came to me when I needed it most and will stay."

⋆ *Reedsy Discovery (Critic Review)*

"Devastating yet hopeful. A lyrical collection that invites us to survive."

About the Author

Thanh Dinh is a Vietnamese-Canadian poet and writer. Her work explores grief, diaspora, queerness, political memory, and the sacred violence of survival. Her debut collection, *The Smallest God Who Ever Lived*, was named a Top New Release on Amazon and praised for its emotional intensity and lyrical boldness. She is the co-founder of **Writerly Books**, a small press committed to radical, poetic, and diasporic storytelling. *Salt and Ashes* is their second collection, composed as a symphonic elegy for the dispossessed and the divine.

You can connect with me on:
- https://patreon.com/hiddengemmystic
- https://www.facebook.com/writerly.books

Also by Thanh Dinh

Kill My Darling
A lyrical descent into madness, obsession, and ruin.

A brutal, intoxicating love story spiraling into madness, **Kill My Darling** follows Angela—a woman teetering on the edge of grief, guilt, and salvation—as she falls for Bambi Raymond, a rising rap star drowning in drugs, trauma, and blood on his hands. Their affair is raw, obsessive, and sacrificial—built not on trust, but on shared self-destruction.

When Bambi dies, whether by overdose or Angela's own hand, she disposes of his body in a frozen lake and begins to unravel. Haunted by hallucinations, stalked by a mysterious man from Bambi's past, and tormented by her own history of abuse, Angela must face a terrible question: Can you worship someone and still save yourself?

Told through poetic fragments, time shifts, and ghost-soaked memories, this is a gospel of toxic love, burning bright and ending in silence. In the final act, Angela drives into the lake—seeking not forgiveness, but reunion.

Chronicle of A Love Foretold
A boy in love. A mother's fury. A silence that won't last.

Dong has lived his life like a well-written essay: perfect grades, perfect obedience, and not a word out of place. But under the surface simmers everything he can't say—especially the letters he keeps writing to Simon, his vanished first love.

When a stolen night brings the boys back together, a kiss reignites everything. But the world doesn't wait for tender things. And when Dong's mother discovers them, everything he's hidden comes crashing down.

Told through poetic letters, fragments of memory, and aching revelations, *Chronicle of A Love Foretold* is a searing exploration of first love, cultural fracture, and the cost of choosing truth over silence.

Love, Anyways
Fifteen stories. Infinite heartbreak. One truth: love remains, even when everything else falls apart.

In this fierce and introspective collection, Thanh Dinh crafts a mosaic of voices—queer lovers, lost migrants, angry daughters, and philosophical drifters—all wrestling with love amid trauma, absurdity, and existential despair. From a tea shop stained with memory to a library haunted by dead authors, each story burns with poetic grit and emotional defiance. *Love, Anyways* doesn't ask if love survives the wreckage—it shows us how it does, and why we keep reaching for it anyway.

www.ingramcontent.com/pod-product-compliance
Lightning Source LLC
Chambersburg PA
CBHW040246010526
44119CB00057B/835